Land of Liberty

Mississippi

by **Kathleen W. Deady**

Consultant:
Bradley G. Bond
Associate Professor
University of Southern Mississippi
Hattiesburg, Mississippi

Capstone
press
Mankato, Minnesota

Capstone Press
151 Good Counsel Drive • P.O. Box 669 • Mankato, Minnesota 56002
http://www.capstone-press.com

Library of Congress Cataloging-in-Publication Data
Deady, Kathleen W.
    Mississippi/by Kathleen W. Deady.
    p. cm.—(Land of liberty)
    Includes bibliographical references and index.
    Contents: About Mississippi—Land, climate, and wildlife—History of
Mississippi—Government and politics—Economy and resources—People and culture.
    ISBN 0-7368-2182-1
    1. Mississippi——Juvenile literature. [1. Mississippi.] I. Title. II. Series.
F341.3.D43 2004
976.2—dc21   2002154954

Summary: An introduction to the geography, history, government, politics, economy,
resources, people, and culture of Mississippi, including maps, charts, and a recipe.

Editorial Credits
Donald Lemke, editor; Jennifer Schonborn, series and book designer; Enoch Peterson,
    illustrator; Kelly Garvin, photo researcher; Eric Kudalis, product planning editor

Photo Credits
Cover images: Stanton Hall, Houserstock Inc./Jan Butchofsky; Mississippi River, Tom
Till Photography/Tom Till

Ann & Rob Simpson, 57; Bruce Coleman Inc./Brian Miller, 17; Bruce Coleman
Inc./C. C. Lockwood, 12; Bruce Coleman Inc./Hans Reinhard, 45; Bruce Coleman
Inc./John Elk III, 14–15, 31, 32; Bruce Coleman Inc./R.E. Pelham, 56; Bruce
Coleman Inc./Robert P. Carr, 8; Capstone Press/Gary Sundermeyer, 54;
Corbis/Bettmann, 16, 37; Corbis Sygma, 43; David Frazier, 26, 38; Folio
Inc./Richard Cummins, 63; GeoImagery Association/J & D Richardson, 4; Getty
Images/Hulton Archive, 53; Houserstock Inc./Dave G. Houser, 40–41; Houserstock
Inc./Jan Butchofsky, 23; Index Stock Imagery/Henry K. Kaiser, 1; Natchez
Convention & Visitors Bureau, 50–51; North Wind Picture Archives, 18, 20, 27, 58;
One Mile Up Inc., 55 (both); Robertstock/R. Krubner, 46; Rutherford B. Hayes
Presidential Center, 29; Stock Montage Inc., 24–25; U.S. Postal Service, 59

Artistic Effects
Comstock, Corbis, Digital Vision, PhotoDisc Inc.

1 2 3 4 5 6 08 07 06 05 04 03

Table of Contents

The Mississippi River Bridge crosses over the Mississippi River near Greenville.

Chapter 1

About Mississippi

The state of Mississippi gets its name from the Mississippi River. This powerful river flows along the state's western border. The river is a major transportation route, tourist attraction, and home to countless plants and animals. Its deep, muddy waters spread more than 1 mile (1.6 kilometers) wide in some places. At 2,350 miles (3,780 kilometers) long, the Mississippi is also the third longest river in the world.

The Mississippi River has played a major role in shaping both Mississippi and the United States. It has been important for transportation since American Indians first settled in the area. The river is also an important trade route, with major ports at Natchez, Vicksburg, and Greenville.

The Magnolia State

Mississippi is a colorful, mostly rural state. Country roads take motorists past forests, farmlands, and green pastures. Flowering magnolia trees fill the air with their scent. The magnolia is the state tree and its white blossom is the state flower. For these reasons, Mississippi is nicknamed the Magnolia State.

Mississippi is located in the southeastern United States. This area is known as the Deep South. Alabama shares Mississippi's eastern border. Tennessee lies to the north. Arkansas is across the Mississippi River to the northwest. Louisiana borders Mississippi to the south and southwest.

Part of Mississippi's southern border is along the Gulf of Mexico. This border is known as the Gulf Coast. A string of islands off the coast is also part of Mississippi.

Mississippi is smaller in size and less populated than many states. It is the 32nd largest state with a total size of 48,434 square miles (125,444 square kilometers). According to the 2000 U.S. Census, 2,844,658 people live in Mississippi. It is the 31st most populated state.

Mississippi Cities

TENNESSEE

ARKANSAS

Pickwick Lake

Oxford ●

Tupelo ●

MISSISSIPPI

Mississippi River

Columbus ●

● Greenwood

Louisville ●

● Greenville

● Belzoni

Philadelphia ●

Mississippi Band
of Choctaw
Indians

Meridian ●

● Vicksburg

☆ Jackson

Forest ●

Pearl River

ALABAMA

● Natchez

● Laurel

● Hattiesburg

LOUISIANA

Biloxi Pascagoula
Gulfport ● ● ●

GULF ISLANDS
NATIONAL SEASHORE

Gulf of Mexico

Legend

▢	American Indian Reservation
✪	Capital
●	City
▱	Lake
〜	River

N
W E
S

Scale
Miles
0   20   40   60   80
0   20   40   60   80
Kilometers

The Mississippi River cuts through rolling hills and valleys in the western part of the state.

Chapter 2

Land, Climate, and Wildlife

Mississippi's rich soil and mild climate create excellent growing conditions. A wide variety of colorful trees and shrubs grow throughout the state. They provide a natural beauty to the people of Mississippi and a home for many types of animals.

Two natural land areas divide the flat plains and gently rolling hills of Mississippi. They are the Mississippi Floodplain and the Eastern Gulf Coastal Plain.

"Mississippi is a lush, pleasant place to live, provided one enjoys the languor of a subtropical climate, flowers, kindness and a relaxed atmosphere."

> —*Pearl S. Buck,* America, *1971, writing about life in Mississippi*

Mississippi Floodplain

The Mississippi Floodplain is a narrow strip of land in the western part of the state. It runs along the east side of the Mississippi River. In the south, the floodplain is only a few miles wide. North of Vicksburg, the floodplain widens into an area called the Delta. The Delta lies along the Mississippi. This area stretches to Tennessee in the north.

The Mississippi Floodplain is part of the Alluvial Plain. For thousands of years the Mississippi River has flooded, dumping rich black soil from upriver. Alluvial soil makes the Delta one of the most important farming areas in the country. Farmers grow much of the country's cotton and soybeans in the Delta.

Eastern Gulf Coastal Plain

The Eastern Gulf Coastal Plain covers the rest of the state. A mixture of lowlands, prairies, forests, and hills cover most of this region. Woodall Mountain, the state's highest point, is also

Mississippi's Land Features

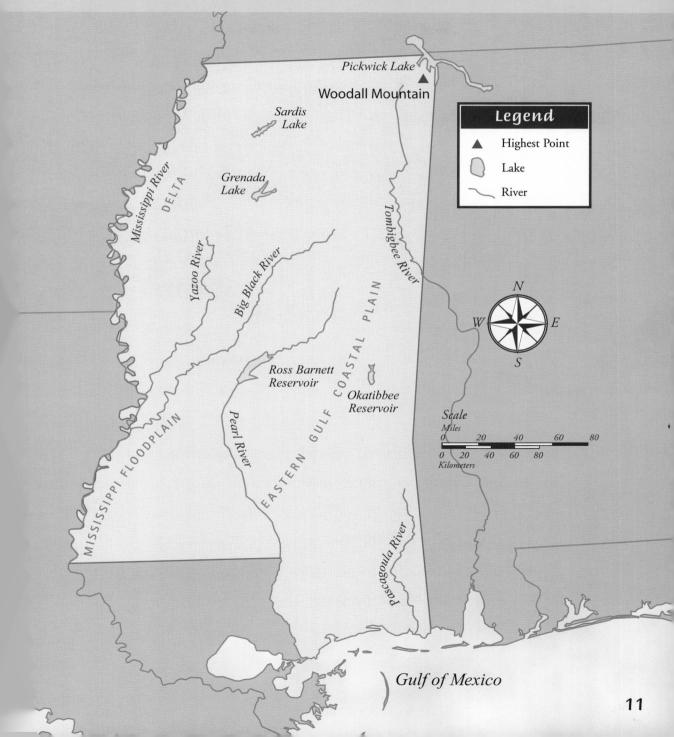

Pickwick Lake

▲ Woodall Mountain

Sardis Lake

Grenada Lake

Mississippi River

DELTA

Yazoo River

Big Black River

Tombigbee River

EASTERN GULF COASTAL PLAIN

MISSISSIPPI FLOODPLAIN

Ross Barnett Reservoir

Okatibbee Reservoir

Pearl River

Pascagoula River

Legend

▲ Highest Point

⬭ Lake

〰 River

Scale
Miles
0   20   40   60   80
0 20 40 60 80
Kilometers

N
W   E
S

Gulf of Mexico

Sea oats and pine trees grow on Horn Island. The island is part of the Gulf Islands National Seashore and a federal wilderness area.

part of the Coastal Plain. At only 806 feet (246 meters) above sea level, Woodall Mountain is more like a hill than a mountain.

The Gulf Coast is at the southern end of the Coastal Plain. Sandy beaches spread along the many bays and coves of the Gulf Coast. Mississippi's lowest point is at sea level along the shore of the Gulf of Mexico.

Rivers and Lakes

Many rivers flow through Mississippi. Several rivers in the western and northern areas of the state feed into the Mississippi River. These include the Yazoo and Big Black Rivers. Many rivers in the eastern part of the state empty into the Gulf of Mexico. They include the Pearl, Pascagoula, and Tombigbee Rivers.

Mississippi also has many reservoirs. River dams created these bodies of water. Reservoirs help control flooding and provide water for the people of Mississippi. In the 1960s, the Ross Barnett Reservoir was built on the Pearl River. It was named after the state's governor at the time.

In 1930, the U.S. government changed the path of the Mississippi. They built dams on several curves of the river to cut off most of the water flow. These dams straightened the main path of the river and improved shipping traffic. The old river curves became oxbow lakes.

Mississippi also has many swampy wetland areas. Slow-moving streams called bayous flow through these marshy areas. These streams include Bayou Chitto and Bayou Pierre. Some bayous connect lakes with the rivers in the Delta. Others connect the inland waters to the Gulf of Mexico.

Climate

Summers in Mississippi are long and hot. In July, temperatures average about 81 degrees Fahrenheit (27 degrees Celsius) statewide. Much of the state has many days that reach 100 degrees Fahrenheit (38 degrees Celsius) in July and August. The breeze off the Gulf of Mexico can keep parts of the southeast coast a little cooler.

Winters are usually short and mild. January temperatures average around 46 degrees Fahrenheit (8 degrees Celsius) across

Bayous in the Gulf Islands National Seashore connect inland waters with the Gulf of Mexico. More than 80 percent of Gulf Islands National Seashore is under water.

the state. Long periods of freezing temperatures are rare, giving farmers a long growing season.

Mississippi's climate is also very moist. The southeast Gulf Coast area receives about 65 inches (165 centimeters) of rain each year. About 50 inches (127 centimeters) of rain falls in the northwest. In winter, small amounts of snow and sleet can fall in northern Mississippi.

Mississippi has many types of storms. Thunder, lightning, hail, and fog sometimes occur with rainstorms. Rare ice

Hurricanes

Hurricanes cross the Gulf of Mexico in late summer and fall. These storms bring high winds, rain, thunder, and lightning. Hurricanes sometimes reach Mississippi's coast.

One of the worst hurricanes to hit Mississippi was Hurricane Camille on August 17, 1969. Winds up to 210 miles (338 kilometers) per hour turned over cars, flattened crops, and uprooted trees. Huge waves destroyed homes and businesses. Over two days, Camille killed 258 people and caused 1.5 billion dollars in damage in the southern United States.

storms may cause millions of dollars in crop damage. Both hurricanes and tornadoes also occur in Mississippi.

Wildlife

The wooded areas of Mississippi support a wide variety of animals. White-tailed deer are the largest common mammals in the state. Other smaller animals include foxes, opossum, raccoons, and armadillos.

Mississippi swamps are filled with many rare and endangered animals, including loggerhead turtles and sand hill cranes. Alligators are also found in the swamps of central and southern Mississippi.

Mississippi has many freshwater and saltwater fish. Freshwater lakes and rivers are filled with catfish, black bass, and carp. In the Gulf of Mexico, mackerel, spotted sea trout, flounder, and tarpon are common. Crabs, shrimp, and oysters are also found along the coast.

Alligators live in swampy areas of central and southern Mississippi.

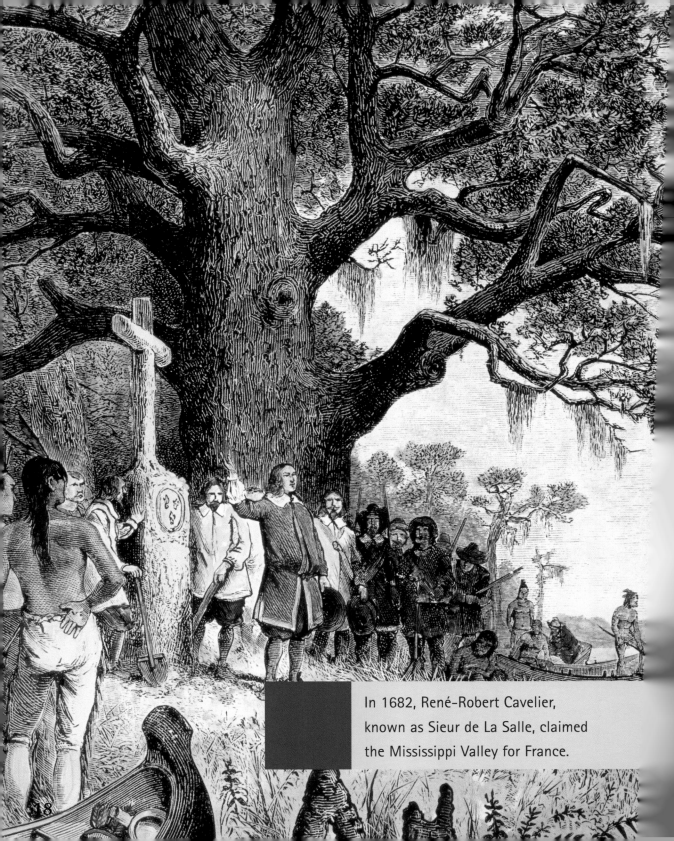

In 1682, René-Robert Cavelier, known as Sieur de La Salle, claimed the Mississippi Valley for France.

Chapter 3

History of Mississippi

American Indians lived in the Mississippi area long before the arrival of European explorers. By 1500, three main tribes ruled the region. The Chickasaw lived in the north and east. The Choctaw were in the central part of the state. The Natchez lived in the southwest along the Mississippi River.

In 1540, Spanish explorer Hernando de Soto passed through the Mississippi area in search of gold. De Soto failed to find any riches. Few people explored the area for about another 140 years.

Then in 1682, French explorer René-Robert Cavelier, known as Sieur de La Salle, traveled the Mississippi River to the Gulf Coast. He claimed the Mississippi Valley for France. La Salle named this huge area Louisiana after King Louis XIV of France.

Pierre Le Moyne, known as Sieur d'Iberville, built the first settlement in the Mississippi area.

Early Settlement and Land Disputes

In 1699, Pierre Le Moyne, known as Sieur d'Iberville, built the first European settlement in the area at Fort Maurepas. Today, this site is the town of Ocean Springs. In 1716, Jean-Baptiste Le Moyne, known as Sieur de Bienville, started a second settlement at Fort Rosalie, now Natchez.

French colonists in the Mississippi area built large farms called plantations. The colonists grew tobacco on these plantations. They also grew indigo, which was used to make blue dye. In 1719, the French brought the first slaves from West Africa to help grow and harvest these crops.

Over time, problems developed between colonists and Indian tribes over control of the land. The Natchez Indians fought several battles with the French in the early 1700s. By 1730, the French had defeated the Natchez, nearly wiping out the entire tribe.

France and Great Britain also argued over control of the land. These problems grew into the French and Indian War (1754–1763). Chickasaw Indians helped the British defeat the French in 1763. Great Britain gained control of most of the land east of the Mississippi River.

Becoming a State

During the Revolutionary War (1775–1783), the American colonies fought for independence against British control. Even after the United States defeated the British, southern land east of the Mississippi River still had few settlers.

In 1798, Congress established the Mississippi Territory. Many settlers soon moved into the area to farm. Cotton became a major crop. By 1817, about 25,000 whites, 23,000 slaves from Africa, and 35,000 American Indians lived in the territory.

Because of this population growth, Mississippi had enough people to become a state. They applied for statehood and became the 20th state on December 10, 1817. Territorial Governor David Holmes became the first state governor. Jackson became the capital in 1822.

By 1830, the population of settlers grew to more than 136,000 in the new state. Pressure grew on the Indians to leave the area. On May 26, 1830, Congress passed the Indian Removal Act. This act gave the government power to move the Indians to Indian Territory in what is now Oklahoma.

After many arguments, the Choctaw agreed to leave. Only about 100 families stayed and were given land. Their descendants still live on a small reservation in Mississippi.

Antebellum Mansions

Before the Civil War, Mississippi was one of the wealthiest states in the country. Rich plantation owners lived like royalty in huge mansions.

Today, many antebellum mansions remain throughout the state. Natchez alone has more than 600 pre-Civil War mansions. This is more than any other southern city. About 100 of these homes are registered landmarks open to the public.

On October 20, 1832, the Chickasaw signed the Treaty of Pontotoc Creek. They turned over their land and moved west to the Indian Territory.

Slavery and States' Rights

As thousands of farmers moved west looking for land, more slaves were brought to work on plantations. By 1860, Mississippi's population was nearly 800,000. More than half of these people were African American slaves.

Cotton made Mississippi one of the wealthiest states. Some rich plantation owners built large homes. Many plantation owners also controlled much of the state government and economy.

During these years, old disagreements grew between the states. Many northerners thought slavery was wrong. Also, northern industries did not use slaves. Northern states thought the government should prevent the spread of slavery to new western states.

Mississippi, like most southern states, disagreed with the northern states. Most Mississippians did not own slaves. But many people believed that large plantations needed slaves to care for and harvest crops. Southerners wanted to keep the right to decide the fate of slavery within their own state borders.

The Civil War

On January 9, 1861, Mississippi was the second state to secede or leave the Union after South Carolina. Nine more southern states followed. They formed the Confederate States of America. Mississippi Senator Jefferson Davis became the president of the Confederacy. The Civil War began in Charleston, South Carolina, on April 12, 1861.

One of the most important battles in Mississippi took place on May 16, 1863. Union soldiers defeated the Confederate army at the Battle of Champion Hill.

Union soldiers, dressed in blue, attacked Confederate soldiers in the Battle of Champion Hill on May 16, 1863. Almost 7,000 soldiers died.

Vicksburg

The Vicksburg National Cemetery is the largest Civil War cemetery in the country. The 116-acre (47-hectare) cemetery is the final resting place for 17,000 Union soldiers. It is the second largest national cemetery. Only Arlington National Cemetery in Virginia is larger.

This victory helped the North gain control of Vicksburg and the Mississippi River. On April 9, 1865, the South surrendered and the war was finally over.

Mississippi suffered terrible losses from the war. Almost half of the state's 78,000 soldiers died. Many more lost an arm or a leg. The war destroyed railroads, buildings, and Mississippi's economy.

Reconstruction

After the Civil War, the northern states helped Mississippi rebuild. This was called Reconstruction. The U.S. government also freed southern slaves and gave them equal rights.

Many white people in the South were angry over the northern control. Mississippi passed laws that denied rights to African Americans. These laws were known as Black Codes. The United States would not let Mississippi become a state again until they followed U.S. laws. Mississippi agreed and rejoined the Union on February 23, 1870.

After rejoining the Union, Mississippi allowed African Americans to vote and go to school. Many were elected to the state legislature. Beginning in 1870, Hiram Rhoades Revels served as the first African American in the U.S. Senate.

On February 25, 1870, Hiram Rhoades Revels became the first African American member of the U.S. Senate.

Racial problems still existed in Mississippi. Many whites did not want to share political power with African Americans. Groups such as the Ku Klux Klan secretly grew. Members of these groups threatened and even killed African Americans.

During the 1880s, Mississippi passed laws to keep African Americans and whites separate. African Americans and whites could not use the same restaurants and bathrooms or go to the same schools. By 1890, the state wrote a new constitution. It denied African Americans many civil rights, including the right to vote.

Slow Change

Although the economy improved in many states at the turn of the century, change was slow in Mississippi. Many whites and African Americans remained poor. By the 1920s, incomes in Mississippi were far lower than the rest of the country. Most Mississippians farmed land that belonged to other people. These sharecroppers gave most of the crop to the landowners as payment for rent.

During the Great Depression (1929–1939), the entire country suffered huge losses. Many Mississippians lost their farms. In addition, insects destroyed much of the cotton crops

Members of the Ku Klux Klan often wore white hoods for disguise, as shown in this 1868 photo. Klan members threatened and killed African Americans in Mississippi and other southern states.

throughout the south. Mississippi realized it could not rely on one crop to support the state's economy.

Business leaders began to develop new industries. During World War II (1941–1945), Ingalls Shipyard in Pascagoula built ships for the Navy. Keesler Air Force Base opened in

1941 in Biloxi to train pilots. Many workers left farming to work in industries and on military bases. Mississippi's economy began to improve.

Civil Rights Movement

After World War II, new attitudes surfaced. African Americans had served their country in the war. They began to protest and demand equal rights. The Civil Rights movement grew.

In 1954, the U.S. Supreme Court ruled that public school segregation was illegal. In 1962, riots began when African American James Meredith tried to enroll in the University of Mississippi. Finally, he was admitted as the university's first African American student in October 1962.

Around the country, pressure was building for Mississippi and other southern states to change. In 1965, President Lyndon B. Johnson signed the Voting Rights Act. This new law forced southern states to allow all races to vote.

A Promising Future

Since 1990, hundreds of corporations, high-tech companies, and research centers have brought new jobs to Mississippi. The John C. Stennis Space Center (SSC) in Hancock County develops equipment for the NASA space program. In 2001, SSC was picked as the site for the Space-Based Laser Test Facility. The space laser may one day help defend the country from an enemy missile attack.

At StenniSphere, Stennis Space Center's visitor center, people can view real rocket engines, train to land a space shuttle, or go inside a model of the International Space Station.

Completed in 1903, the state capitol in Jackson serves as the center of government in Mississippi.

Chapter 4

Government and Politics

Mississippi has had six constitutions. Each constitution is related to an important event in the state's history. On December 17, 1817, Mississippi adopted its first constitution and became the 20th state. In 1832, the second constitution gave all white males the right to vote. After seceding from the Union in 1861, Mississippi adopted a third constitution. This document lasted until the end of the Civil War.

After the Civil War in 1865, a fourth constitution ended slavery in the state. In 1869, a fifth constitution allowed Mississippi to reenter the Union. It also gave former slaves the same rights as whites, including the right to vote. More than 20 years later, the state adopted a sixth constitution. It prevented

African Americans from voting. This 1890 constitution is still in use, but has had many amendments.

State Government

Mississippi's government is similar to the structure of the federal government. The state government is made up of executive, legislative, and judicial branches.

The executive branch enforces the laws and runs the state's business. The governor heads the executive branch. The governor may serve any number of four-year terms, but not more than two in a row.

The legislative branch includes both the senate and the house of representatives. The senate has 52 members and the house of representatives has 122 members. The legislative branch makes the laws for the state. Members of the legislative branch are elected to four-year terms.

Mississippi's State Government

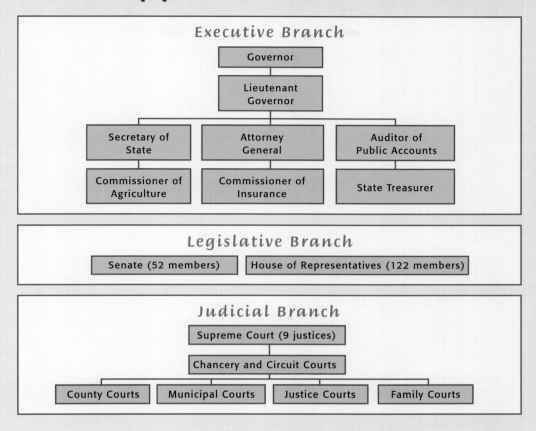

Executive Branch

- Governor
- Lieutenant Governor
  - Secretary of State
  - Attorney General
  - Auditor of Public Accounts
  - Commissioner of Agriculture
  - Commissioner of Insurance
  - State Treasurer

Legislative Branch

- Senate (52 members)
- House of Representatives (122 members)

Judicial Branch

- Supreme Court (9 justices)
- Chancery and Circuit Courts
  - County Courts
  - Municipal Courts
  - Justice Courts
  - Family Courts

The judicial branch is made up of many courts. The highest court in Mississippi is the supreme court. There are nine members elected to the supreme court. Other lower courts include circuit courts, county courts, municipal courts, and family courts.

Voting Rights

During the civil rights movement of the 1950s and 1960s, African Americans demanded equal rights. They protested individually and in groups to bring about change.

The Voting Rights Act of 1965 changed unfair voting laws in the south. It gave all African Americans in Mississippi the right to vote. Soon, African Americans were affecting election results. They were able to elect African Americans to government positions. In 1969, Charles Evers was elected as mayor of Fayette, Mississippi. Evers was the first African American mayor in Mississippi since Reconstruction.

Political Parties

Throughout most of its history, Mississippi has been a Democratic state. From 1876 to 1944, Mississippians elected Democrats in every local, state, and national election.

After World War II, civil rights began affecting politics. Democrats often supported equal rights for all races. White voters began to vote against Democrats. After the Voting Rights Act of 1965, African Americans began to register and vote. They mostly voted for Democrats.

On August 19, 1971, the mayor of Fayette, Charles Evers, spoke to a crowd of Mississippians. Evers and his brother Medgar were leaders in the struggle for civil rights. Medgar was assassinated in 1963.

In recent years, Mississippi has changed to a strong Republican state. Huge numbers of white voters have been voting for Republican leaders. In 1978, Thad Cochran was elected the first Republican U.S. senator from Mississippi since Reconstruction. In 1988, Republican Trent Lott was also elected to the senate. In 1991, Kirk Fordice was elected the state's first Republican governor in 120 years.

Cotton is harvested in the Delta. It is one of Mississippi's leading agricultural products.

Chapter 5

Economy and Resources

For many years, Mississippi's economy was based almost completely on cotton farming. In the 1930s, insects called boll weevils destroyed much of the cotton crop in the state. Mississippi realized it could not depend on one farm crop.

In 1936, Governor Hugh White started a program called Balance Agriculture with Industry. The program helped new industries get started in Mississippi and brought jobs for local workers.

Service Industries

Today, service industries combine to make up the largest part of Mississippi's economy. Service workers include people in sales, real estate, banking and investment, insurance, and government services. They also include workers in health care and education.

Jackson is the center of finance and government in Mississippi. Large insurance and real estate companies have their main offices in the capital city. Many government workers have jobs in Jackson. Government employees provide services in schools, hospitals, social service agencies, and on military bases.

Two riverboats, the *Mississippi Queen* and the *Delta Queen*, float along the Mississippi River. People on the riverboats enjoy food, entertainment, and gambling.

Tourism

Tourism is an important service industry in Mississippi. Hunters and fishers come to the state from around the world. Mississippi has more than 1 million acres (405,000 hectares) of excellent game hunting land. In addition, state reservoirs have some of the best bass fishing in the country.

Mississippi has many other attractions. Riverboat casinos on the Mississippi River and Gulf Coast bring people and money to the state. Large southern mansions are favorite tourist spots.

Many people visit national parks like Natchez Trace Park and Gulf Islands National Seashore.

Manufacturing and Mining

Manufacturing makes up the second largest part of Mississippi's economy. Many factories process meats and seafood. Poultry from farms is processed in large plants in Forest and Laurel. Other food products include dairy products, baked goods, beverages, and seasonings.

Mississippians make many products from the state's natural resources. Workers produce petroleum in the southern corners of the state. Mississippi has valuable deposits of natural gas. Workers use many kinds of clay to make products like bricks and tiles. Other mineral products include sand, gravel, iron ore, limestone, and salt.

The state also makes many products from wood. Columbus, Laurel, Louisville, and Vicksburg have large wood processing plants. Workers build furniture from hardwoods such as hickory and oak. Other wood products include lumber, paper, particleboard, and fiberboard.

On December 13, 2002, the USS *Cole* arrived at Litton shipyard aboard a commercial lift ship. Several months earlier, terrorists in Yemen bombed the *Cole*. Litton Ingalls Shipbuilding agreed to repair the damage.

Mississippi is known as one of the top shipbuilding states. Shipyards along the Gulf Coast make freighters and tankers, including ships for the U.S. Navy and Merchant Marine. The largest shipbuilder is Litton Ingalls Shipbuilding in Pascagoula.

Agriculture and Fishing

Agriculture is still important to the state's economy. In 2001, Mississippi was the country's second largest cotton producer, after Texas. Soybeans have also become a leading crop. Farmers grow hay, corn, sorghum, wheat, rice, and peanuts. Vegetables grown in the state include sweet potatoes, peas, and cucumbers. Leading fruit crops include peaches, watermelons, and grapes.

Livestock and other animal products make up a large part of the state's agriculture. Mississippi produces about 740 million broiler chickens and 1.6 million eggs yearly. Farmers raise beef cattle in most areas except the Delta.

Forestry is a growing area of agriculture. Mississippi grows about 120 varieties of trees. They include several kinds of pine, as well as ash, cypress, elm, hickory, and oak trees. In 2001, wood was the leading agricultural crop in 40 counties.

In recent years, Mississippi has become the largest producer of catfish in the country. Many old plantation farms have changed to fish hatcheries. The catfish are raised in ponds.

Catfish Farming

Mississippi catfish farming started in the area of Belzoni in the 1960s. Farmers there began digging ponds to raise catfish as a crop. The Delta's flat land, plentiful ground water, and mild climate were perfect for raising catfish.

In recent years, catfish farming has become the state's fastest growing industry. Mississippi has more than 400 catfish farms. These farms have more than 113,000 acres (46,000 hectares) of catfish ponds. Mississippi provides almost 70 percent of the catfish for the United States.

Every day, workers ship thousands of catfish to restaurants and supermarkets across the country.

Mississippi's location on the Gulf of Mexico makes it a major producer of seafood as well. Mississippi is the fifth leading state in total pounds of seafood caught. It is also an important shrimp fishing state. Other saltwater fish from the Gulf of Mexico include oysters, mackerel, and red snapper.

Jackson is the capital of Mississippi. The city serves as the center of government and finance in the state.

Chapter 6

People and Culture

Mississippi has always been mainly a rural and agricultural state. In recent years, the farming lifestyle has become less important. More people are working in manufacturing and service industry jobs.

In 1920, around 13 percent of Mississippians lived in urban areas. Soon, many people started moving from the country to towns and cities. By 2000, nearly half of all Mississippi residents lived in urban areas.

Population and Ethnic Diversity

Almost 61 percent of Mississippians are white. That number is the second lowest percentage of whites of any state,

"Later others came to this lower delta—Italians, Irish, Jews, Syrians, even Chinese—to produce a curious melting pot, black, yellow, and white, and all the gradations known to man."
    —Willie Morris ,1934-1999, Mississippi writer, North Toward Home

after Hawaii. Most white Mississippians descend from people who settled in the original 13 colonies. These settlers came from Ireland, Scotland, England, France, Germany, and other European countries. Many of these early settlers moved west and south into Mississippi and neighboring states.

Mississippi also has the highest percentage of African Americans of any state. African Americans make up just over 36 percent of the total population. Mississippi's African American residents mainly descend from slaves brought from Africa in the 1700s and 1800s.

The rest of Mississippi's population comes from many different backgrounds. These include Hispanics and people of varied Asian decent. Many people of Chinese ancestry came to Mississippi in the 1870s. Most Chinese immigrants worked in fields and on plantations, replacing slaves during Reconstruction.

A small population of American Indians, mostly Choctaw, also live in Mississippi. Today, most of the Choctaw Indians live on a small reservation in central Mississippi.

Mississippi's Ethnic Background

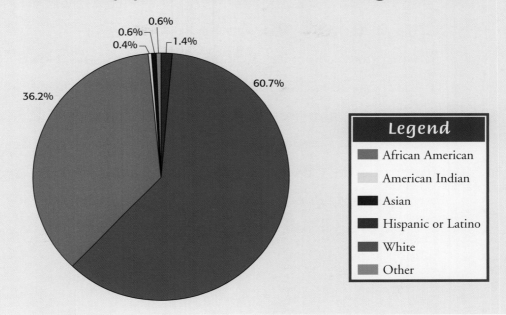

0.6%
0.6%
0.4%
1.4%
60.7%
36.2%

Legend
- African American
- American Indian
- Asian
- Hispanic or Latino
- White
- Other

Hospitality State

Mississippi has long been called the Hospitality State. Most Mississippians are proud of their friendliness and good manners. Many people in the state will go out of their way to greet people and offer help.

This relaxed friendliness can be seen throughout the state. Even in Mississippi's largest cities, people take the time to chat. Visitors can ask for simple directions and end up in a friendly conversation with a stranger. Farmers look up from their work to wave at people passing by.

Fairs and Festivals

Mississippians celebrate at many fairs, festivals, and shows. Along the Gulf Coast, Mardi Gras is the biggest party of the year. Mississippi Mardi Gras is filled with parades, music, and dancing. Other events include the Elvis Presley Festival in Tupelo and the Choctaw Indian Fair near Philadelphia. The International Balloon Classic in Greenwood and the Great Mississippi River Balloon Race in Natchez offer popular hot-air balloon shows.

Every October, dozens of hot-air balloons compete in the Great Mississippi River Balloon Race in Natchez.

The Blessing of the Fleet in Biloxi opens shrimp season. This event includes a street festival, a parade of colorful boats, and the crowning of a Shrimp King and Queen.

Mississippi also has many musical events. The Mississippi Blues Festival is in September at the Jackson County Fair. Regionally and nationally known blues, soul, and gospel singers perform at the festival. People can also visit the Blues Museum in Cleveland, Mississippi.

Music and Literature

Many famous musicians were born in Mississippi. Elvis Presley was one of the most popular rock and roll performers of the 1950s and 1960s. He was born in Tupelo. Bo Diddley was also born in Mississippi. He is a well-known guitarist and blues singer. Top stars of today from Mississippi include Lance Bass from *NSYNC, LeAnn Rimes, and Faith Hill.

Many famous writers have also come from Mississippi. William Faulkner was born in New Albany. He won the Nobel Prize in Literature in 1949. He also won the Pulitzer Prize in 1955 and 1963. His most famous work, *The Sound and the Fury*, was written in 1929. Other Mississippi writers include playwright Tennessee Williams and novelist Richard Wright.

In recent decades, Mississippi has probably seen more changes than any other state. Mississippi has overcome slavery, Civil War destruction, and segregation. The people of the Magnolia State will continue to work together and improve their state for the future.

Elvis Presley performed for a crowd in 1957.
Presley was born in Tupelo, Mississippi.

Recipe: Mississippi Mud Cake

This classic chocolate cake is the same color as the deep, rich soil of the Mississippi River. Try this recipe topped with miniature marshmallows.

Ingredients

2 sticks of margarine
4 eggs
½ cup (120 mL) cocoa
1½ cups (360 mL) self-rising
     flour
½ cup (120 mL) milk
1 teaspoon (5 mL) vanilla
dash of salt
2 cups (480 mL) sugar
1½ cups (360 mL) chopped
     pecans
1 10-ounce (275-gram) package
     miniature marshmallows

Equipment

microwave-safe bowl
large mixing bowl
fork
dry-ingredient measuring cups
measuring spoons
liquid measuring cup
electric mixer
large mixing spoon
nonstick cooking spray
9- by 13-inch (23- by 33-centimeter)
     baking pan
oven mitts

What You Do

1. Preheat oven to 350°F (180°C).

2. Place margarine in microwave-safe bowl and heat in microwave for 30 seconds or until margarine is melted.

3. In a large mixing bowl, beat eggs with a fork.

4. Add melted margarine, cocoa, flour, milk, vanilla, salt, and sugar to the large mixing bowl. Beat well with electric mixer until smooth.

5. Stir pecans into mixture with a large mixing spoon.

6. Spray baking pan with nonstick cooking spray.

7. Pour mixture into prepared baking pan and bake for 35 minutes.

8. Remove cake from oven with oven mitts.

9. Pour marshmallows over cake while still hot.

10. Place cake in warm oven until marshmallows are melted.

11. Remove cake from oven with oven mitts and allow to cool before serving.

Makes 12-15 servings

Mississippi's Flag and Seal

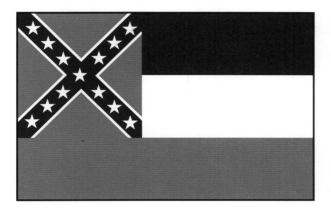

Mississippi's Flag

The state legislature adopted Mississippi's flag in 1894. The flag has three horizontal stripes. The stripes are red, white, and blue, the national colors. A confederate flag is in the upper left corner. It has a blue X outlined in white on a red background. The thirteen white stars on the X stand for the original thirteen colonies.

Mississippi's State Seal

Mississippi adopted its official state seal in 1894. The seal shows an eagle with widespread wings. On the eagle's breast is a shield with stars and stripes. The eagle holds an olive branch in its right talon and three arrows in its left. The olive branch stands for the desire for peace. The arrows represent war. Below the eagle is a single star. The words "The Great Seal of the State of Mississippi" are in a circle around the border.

Almanac

Magnolia

Nickname:
Magnolia State

Population: 2,844,658
(U.S. Census 2000)
Population rank: 31st

Capital: Jackson

Largest cities: Jackson,
Gulfport, Biloxi,
Hattiesburg, Greenville

Area: 48,434 square miles
(125,444 square kilometers)

Size rank: 32nd

Highest point:
Woodall Mountain, 806 feet
(246 meters) above sea level

Lowest point: Gulf Coast,
sea level

Agricultural products:
Poultry, wood, cotton,
catfish, soybeans, rice,
wheat

**Average summer
temperature:**
81 degrees Fahrenheit
(27 degrees Celsius)

**Average winter
temperature:**
46 degrees Fahrenheit
(8 degrees Celsius)

**Average annual
precipitation:** 56 inches
(142 centimeters)

Natural resources:
Petroleum, natural gas, sand and gravel, bentonite, chalk, limestone

Types of industry:
Wholesale and retail sales, government services, tourism, shipbuilding

First governor:
David Holmes, 1817–1820

Statehood:
December 17, 1817 (20th state)

U.S. Representatives: 4

U.S. Senators: 2

U.S. electoral votes: 6

Counties: 82

Bird: Mockingbird

Dance: Square dance

Flower: Magnolia

Fossil: Prehistoric whale

Shell: Oyster shell

Song: "Go, Mississippi," by Houston Davis

Tree: Magnolia

Waterfowl: Wood duck

Wood duck

Timeline

State History

1500
Chickasaw, Choctaw, and Natchez Indians live in the area that is now Mississippi.

1540
Spanish explorer Hernando de Soto reaches Mississippi while searching for gold.

1699
Frenchman Pierre Le Moyne starts the first settlement at Fort Maurepas.

1817
Mississippi becomes the 20th state on December 10.

1861
Mississippi becomes the second of 11 states to secede from the Union and form the Confederate States of America.

U.S. History

1620
The Pilgrims establish a colony in North America.

1775–1783
American colonists fight for their independence from Great Britain in the Revolutionary War.

1861–1865
The North and the South fight the Civil War.

1914–1918
World War I is fought; the United States enters the war in 1917.

1936

Governor Hugh White starts Balance Agriculture with Industry program.

1962

James Meredith enrolls as the first African American student at the University of Mississippi.

1991

Mississippi elects Kirk Fordice as their first Republican governor in 120 years.

2001

Stennis Space Center is picked as the site for the Space-Based Laser Performance Test Facility.

1939–1945

World War II is fought; the United States enters the war in 1941.

1964

The U.S. Congress passes the Civil Rights Act, which makes discrimination illegal.

2001

On September 11, terrorists attack the World Trade Center and the Pentagon.

1929–1939

The United States experiences the Great Depression.

Words to Know

alluvial (ah-LOO-vee-ahl)—made from soil carried and left by a river

antebellum (an-tee-BELL-um)—existing before the Civil War

bayou (BYE-oo)—a stream that runs slowly through a swamp and leads to or from a lake or river

floodplain (FLUHD-plane)—an area of land near a river or stream that floods during heavy rains

hatchery (HACH-er-ee)—a place where eggs are hatched

oxbow lake (OKS-boh LAKE)—a U-shaped lake formed when a river's path is straightened

plantation (plan-TAY-shuhn)—a large farm where one crop is grown

reservoir (REZ-ur-vwar)—a natural or artificial holding area for a large amount of water

secede (si-SEED)—to withdraw; Mississippi seceded from the United States in 1861.

sharecropper (SHAIR-krop-ur)—a person who works a piece of land for food, shelter, and part of the crops grown

To Learn More

Figueroa, Acton. *Mississippi, the Magnolia State.* World Almanac Library of the States. Milwaukee: World Almanac Library, 2003.

Peacock, Judith. *Reconstruction: Rebuilding after the Civil War.* Let Freedom Ring. Mankato, Minn.: Bridgestone Books, 2003.

Peacock, Judith. *Secession: The Southern States Leave the Union.* Let Freedom Ring. Mankato, Minn.: Bridgestone Books, 2003.

Somervill, Barbara A. *Mississippi.* From Sea to Shining Sea. New York: Children's Press, 2003.

Internet Sites

Do you want to find out more about Mississippi?
Let FactHound, our fact-finding hound dog, do the research for you.

Here's how:
1) Visit *http://www.facthound.com*
2) Type in the **Book ID** number:
   0736821821
3) Click on **FETCH IT.**

FactHound will fetch Internet sites picked by our editors just for you!

Places to Write and Visit

Delta Blues Museum
#1 Blues Alley
P. O. Box 459
Clarksdale, MS 38614

**Mississippi Department of
Wildlife, Fisheries, and Parks**
1505 Eastover Drive
Jackson, MS 39211-6374

Mississippi Division of Tourism
P. O. Box 849
Jackson, MS 39205

Mississippi Forestry Commission
301 North Lamar
Suite 300
Jackson, MS 39201

Mississippi Historical Society
P. O. Box 571
Jackson, MS 39205-0571

Stennis Space Center
NASA Public Affairs
PA00
Stennis Space Center, MS 39529

A shrimp boat rests in Small Craft Harbor in Biloxi. Mississippi is a leading shrimp fishing state.

LUCY F.

63

Index

T 57132

West Union School
23870 NW West Union Road
Hillsboro, Oregon 97124